CONTENTS

CHINA ON THE MAP

China (officially called the People's Republic of China) is an enormous country, the fourth largest in the world by area. More people live there than anywhere else — almost 1.4 billion of them. With awe-inspiring landscapes, colourful festivals, delicious food and buzzing cities, this is a fascinating place to go exploring.

≪ China old and new.

'HUANYING DAO ZHONGGOU!' THAT'S HOW TO SAY 'WELCOME TO CHINA!' IN MANDARIN CHINESE.

C H I N A

China fact file

Population: 1,367,485,388 (July 2015 est.)

Area: 9.6 million sq km

Capital city: Beijing

Highest peak: Mount Everest (8,848m)

Main language: Mandarin Chinese

Currency: Yuan (also called renminbi)

CHINA

Anita Ganeri

The LAND and the PEOPLE

Published in paperback in 2017 by Wayland

Editor: Nicola Edwards
Design: Dave Ball and Angela Ball at D&A
Cover design: D&A
Map artwork by Stefan Chabluk

ISBN: 978 0 7502 9844 5
10 9 8 7 6 5 4 3 2 1

MIX
Paper from
responsible sources
FSC
www.fsc.org
FSC® C104740

Wayland, an imprint of
Hachette Children's Group
Part of Hodder and Stoughton
Carmelite House
50 Victoria Embankment
London EC4Y ODZ

An Hachette UK Company
www.hachette.co.uk
www.hachettechildrens.co.uk

Printed in Singapore

Picture acknowledgements: All images and graphic elements courtesy of Shutterstock
except pp 14t, 15bl, 18b, 29b, 32t, 38b, 40b, 44l and 45r Corbis

Every attempt has been made to clear copyright. Should there be any inadvertent
omission, please apply to the publisher for rectification.

Ancient and modern

In recent years, China has become a powerful force in the world economy but it is also a land of contrasts and extremes. While it continues to grow and develop, it maintains its rich, ancient culture. In the countryside, poor farmers still grow rice in the traditional way, whilst in the cities, super-rich business people work in high-tech offices in gleaming skyscrapers.

Whistlestop China

Top things to do on a tour of China...

⌃ Walk along the Great Wall (see page 30).

⌃ See the Terracotta Army (see page 31).

Beijing • Tianjin

Shanghai

Chongqing

Guangzhou

Shenzhen

⌃ Mainland China is divided into 22 provinces.

⌃ Feast on Peking Duck (see page 35).

« Practise tai chi (see page 38).

5

PEOPLE AND LANGUAGE

With a population approaching 1.4 billion people, China accounts for around one in five of all the people living on Earth. The Chinese are proud of their nation, work hard, and are courteous and generous.

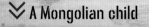

≫ A Mongolian child

A Manchurian woman ≫

Ethnic groups

More than 90 per cent of Chinese people belong to an ethnic group called the Han Chinese. They live mostly in central and eastern China. The rest of China's population is made up of people from more than 50 ethnic minorities, such as Tibetans, Manchus and Mongolians.

A Tibetan girl ≫

6

Famous Chinese

Confucius (551-479 BCE)
Philosopher and politician

Mao Tse Tung (1893-1976)
Communist leader of China

I M Pei (born 1917)
Architect

Zhang Ziyi (born 1979)
Actress and model

Languages and dialects

Nearly 300 different languages are spoken in China, although most people speak one of the seven different dialects of Chinese. Of these dialects, Mandarin is the official language of China. Chinese is written down in characters, not letters, with each character standing for a word or part of a word.

Chinese characters are ≫ written with a brush.

⌄⌄ A Chinese one-child family

MOST CHINESE PEOPLE KNOW BETWEEN 6–8,000 CHARACTERS.

FOCUS ON

☑ POPULATION CONTROL

In 1979, in an effort to stop the population growing too fast to feed itself, the Chinese government introduced a policy that families could only have one child. This remained in place until 2015, when the government announced that parents were now allowed to have two children.

AMAZING LANDSCAPES

China is a huge country with an amazing range of landscapes — from towering mountains and vast deserts in the west, to flood-prone rivers in the east, vast conifer forests and bogs in the north, and palm-fringed tropical beaches in the south.

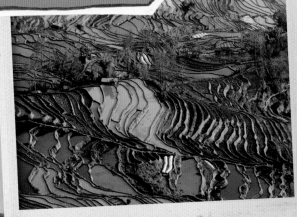

⌃ Spectacular rice-growing terraces on mountainous slopes in Yunnan province.

⌄ The dramatic Huangshan (Yellow Mountains)

Mountains

With two-thirds of the landscape made up of mountains and high plateaus, China is a hilly place. As well as the dramatic peaks of the Himalayas (see page 10), there are dozens of other mountain ranges. Among the most scenic are the Huangshan, or Yellow Mountains, in the east of the country.

⌃ Rushing water at
Tiger Leaping Gorge

THE WULINGYUAN SCENIC AREA IS SAID TO HAVE BEEN THE INSPIRATION FOR THE FLOATING MOUNTAINS IN THE FILM 'AVATAR'

Natural beauty

China has so much beautiful scenery that it is difficult to know where to start. The spectacular Tiger Leaping Gorge, in Yunnan province, is 16km long and up to 2km deep, and offers fine views of snow-capped peaks on both sides. For blue lakes and forested valleys, head for one of the many designated national parks, such as the Jiuzhaigou nature reserve.

FOCUS ON

☑ ROCK TOWERS

One of China's most photographed landscapes is the Wulingyuan Scenic Area in Hunan province (left), where thousands of sandstone towers emerge from misty forests below. Amongst the towers are tumbling rivers, and spectacular caves containing stalactites and stalagmites.

HIGH AND DRY

In the far west of China lies the Tibetan Plateau, a massive area of land up to 5,000 m above sea level, which is sometimes called the 'roof of the world'. To the south of the Tibetan Plateau tower the Himalayas, and to the north lie vast, dry deserts.

⌃ Yaks on Tibetan Plateaus

⌄ View of Everest from China

⌄ The Potala Palace in Lhasa, on the Tibetan Plateau, is a UNESCO world heritage site.

Mighty mountains

The world's highest mountain range, the Himalayas, stretches for around 2,400km and forms the borders between China and Nepal, and China and Bhutan. Star of the show is Mount Everest, the highest peak on the planet, at 8,848m tall. The northern half of the mountain stands in China, and is known locally as Qomolangma, which means 'Holy Mother'.

▼ Pilgrims circumnavigating Mount Kailash.

☑ **MOUNT KAILASH**

Dome-shaped Mount Kailash in eastern China is Asia's most sacred mountain and one of the holiest sites in the world for Buddhists, Hindus and Jains. Despite its remoteness, thousands of people make a pilgrimage to the mountain each year. They believe that walking around its 52km base in an anti-clockwise direction will bring them good fortune.

Deadly deserts

A quarter of China's land area is desert, and most of this lies north of the Tibetan Plateau. China's largest desert, the Taklamakan Desert, is one of the biggest sandy deserts in world, with giant sand dunes that are constantly shifted and re-shaped by the wind. The desert is roasting hot in summer but bitterly cold in winter, with snow on the ground and temperatures dropping below -20°C.

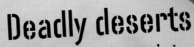

⌃ The sand dunes in the Taklamakan Desert can be up to 150m high.

A TALE OF TWO RIVERS

Running from the high Tibetan Plateau, then across the lowlands of the east and into the sea, are two of China's largest and most iconic rivers – the Yellow River and the Yangtze. Millions of people live along them and on their floodplains, and both rivers have helped to shape Chinese history.

The Yangtze

At 6,300km, the Yangtze (called the Chang Jiang in China) is China's longest river, and the third longest river in the world. It divides China into north and south, and a third of China's population lives in its drainage basin. Sadly, the Yangtze is also one of the world's most polluted rivers because of chemicals from industry and agriculture.

⩔ The mighty Yangtze flows through a deep gorge.

⩘ Huge cruise ships carry hundreds of passengers along the Yangtze River.

⩔ The Yangtze's water is polluted by sewage and industrial waste.

The Yellow River

Second only to the Yangtze, the Yellow River (called the Huang He in China) is 5,463km long. It gets its popular name from the yellow-coloured silt (below) that its water washes downstream. Prone to devastating floods which have killed millions of people, the Yellow River is also known as 'China's Sorrow'.

IN 1931, ONE OF THE YELLOW RIVER'S WORST RECORDED FLOODS KILLED AN ESTIMATED MILLION PEOPLE.

>> Raging flood waters on the Yellow River

FOCUS ON

☑ ### THE THREE GORGES DAM

Constructed between 1992 and 2009, the Three Gorges Dam is the world's biggest dam. It was built to produce electricity for China's growing cities and industries (it is the most powerful hydroelectric station in the world), and for flood control. The dam is controversial because dozens of cities, towns and historic sites were flooded to create its reservoir.

⌄ The controversial Three Gorges Dam

PANDA-MANIA

China is home to some extremely rare animals. However, habitat destruction, pollution, and the demand for animal parts to make traditional medicines have placed many species in grave danger.

≫ Giant pandas are the national symbol of China.

A NEWBORN GIANT PANDA CUB IS JUST ONE NINE HUNDREDTH THE SIZE OF ITS MOTHER.

≪ A mother panda with her tiny cub

Giant panda

China's famous giant panda is only found in bamboo forests, which supply its favourite food. Its habitat has been devastated through logging, and it is now one of the most endangered bears in the world. Fewer than 2,000 survive in the wild, mostly on reserves, but the good news is that the numbers of giant pandas are increasing. At the Chengdu Panda Base in Sichuan, giant pandas are being bred in captivity, then reintroduced into the wild.

South China tiger

Sixty years ago, thousands of these beautiful creatures lived in forests in China but were hunted in such large numbers that they may now be extinct in the wild. Some are found in zoos but all were born in captivity.

<< A pair of red-crowned cranes

^ South China tiger cubs

Baiji

The Baiji, or Yangtze River dolphin, was officially declared extinct in 2006 when an expedition failed to find any. Its decline was blamed on river pollution, becoming entangled in fishing nets, and collisions with boats.

⌄ The now-extinct Baiji in the Yangtze River

Red-crowned crane

A symbol of luck and a long life, the red-crowned crane is named after the bare patch of red skin on its head. Its wetland nests on the lower reaches of the Yangtze have been disappearing, but now nature reserves are being set up to help protect the red-crowned crane's habitats and breeding areas.

FOCUS ON

☑ CHINESE MEDICINES

Some animal parts, such as tiger bones and rhinoceros horn, are used in traditional Chinese medicine. The demand has contributed to many species becoming endangered. Among them is the Chinese alligator, whose meat is believed to cure colds and prevent cancer.

WORKING THE LAND

With so many mountains, flat lowland suitable for farming is in short supply in China. In fact, only about 15 per cent of the land can be used for growing crops. Even so, Chinese farmers, working mostly on small family farms, produce enough food to feed a fifth of the world's population.

⌃ Nomadic herders move from place to place with their goats.

⌃ Paddy fields on the outskirts of a city – an example of urban farming.

Rice growing

Rice is China's main crop, and its staple food. It is grown in paddy fields that are ploughed, levelled, and then flooded with water. Seedlings are planted, and the crop is ready to harvest after just three to four months. Between three and four rice crops are grown each year.

RICE IS NOT ONLY EATEN IN GRAIN FORM, BUT IS ALSO MADE INTO WINE, FLOUR, PAPER AND NOODLES.

FOCUS ON

✓ TERRACED PADDIES

In China's hilly countryside, farmers can't grow rice on sloping hillsides because it would be impossible to flood the crops. Instead, they build narrow, flat terraces with earth banks to contain the water. Rows and rows of terraced paddy fields are a common sight in China.

⯅ Terraced paddy fields on a sloping mountain side

⯆ Farmers plant rice seedlings in a paddy field.

Tea time

Other important crops include wheat, barley, potatoes, citrus and tropical fruits, and tea. Tea growers produce many varieties of tea, such as green tea, black tea, and jasmine tea. Almost a third of the world's tea comes from China, mostly from the south and east of the country.

≪ A skilled tea picker plucks leaves from the plant without damaging them.

NATURAL RICHES

Famous for its silk, cotton and bamboo, China is rich in natural resources. It also has large amounts of minerals, such as coal, iron, tin, copper, lead and zinc.

⌃ Drilling derricks at an iron mine in Hebei province

⌄ Smoke belches out from the coal-burning Datong power station in Shanxi province.

AT 12 PER CENT, CHINA HAS THE THIRD-LARGEST PERCENTAGE OF THE WORLD'S MINERAL RESOURCES, AFTER THE USA AND RUSSIA.

Coal production

China produces around 3.5 billion tonnes of coal a year, more than any other country and almost half the world's total. Incredibly, China uses all of this, and imports more, to feed its hundreds of coal-guzzling power stations. These produce most of the electricity needed for its growing cities and factories.

Bamboo

Bamboo-growing is a flourishing industry in China. There are natural bamboo forests, and bamboo is also grown on plantations. Bamboo grows very quickly, and shoots can be harvested after just a year or two. It is made into dozens of objects, from chopsticks (below right) to scaffolding, and is processed to make paper, textiles and medicines.

⌃ Workers load bamboo to be used in building on to a cart.

FOCUS ON

✓ SILK PRODUCTION

Silk has been made in China since ancient times. It is woven from the very fine fibres of silkworm cocoons — the caterpillars of the Chinese silkworm moth. The Chinese discovered silk-making around 4,700 years ago, and kept it secret for more than 3,000 years.

≪ These workers are making silk in a factory in Suzhou, in Jiangsu province. Silk production is a painstaking process, and is still done mostly by hand.

MADE IN CHINA

In recent years, China has become the world's largest economy, and the biggest global manufacturer of electronic goods, toys and shoes. It also has the world's biggest workforce, with people working longer and for less pay than in the West.

⌃ A container ship in Shanghai is loaded with goods for export.

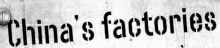

China's factories

One reason for China's growth is that its companies have invested in cutting-edge manufacturing technology and in training their workers to use it. The result is that companies from all over the world have moved their factories to cities, such as Chengdu (above), a centre for electronics. More than a third of Apple iPads, and half of Intel microchips, are made here.

⌃ Workers on an assembly line at a factory in Shenzhen which produces surveillance camera equipment.

Communism and shopping

China is a communist country. This means that the state owns the country's companies and factories, and sets the level of wages and the prices of goods in the shops. But the Chinese government does now allow people to own their own businesses. As the Chinese economy has grown, so has the number of middle-class people in the country, as well as shops where they can spend the money they have made.

Shiny new shopping malls have sprung up in many Chinese cities.

FOCUS ON

☑ **TOY MAKERS**

Take a look at a plastic toy and you'll most likely find that it has MADE IN CHINA stamped on it somewhere. Chinese companies have become experts at making toys cheaply, together producing a staggering 90 per cent of the world's toys.

≫ A motorcycle becomes a mobile shop packed with 'Made in China' toys!

THREE QUARTERS OF ALL THE TOYS SOLD IN THE USA ARE MADE IN CHINA.

ENVIRONMENT IN DANGER

The downside of China's economic success is the damage being done to the environment. Pollution of air and water, caused by emissions and effluents from power stations and factories, as well as desertification and habitat loss, are having a devastating effect.

⌄ Power stations belch chemicals into the air.

⌄ The polluted water of Lake Taihu

⌄ Industrial waste pollutes river water.

Water pollution

Laws around water pollution are not well observed in China, and there are frequent accidental spillages of chemicals from factories into rivers. Effluent creates a cocktail of chemicals that kills aquatic life, and makes water undrinkable. Even underground water supplies are contaminated by chemicals that seep down through the soil.

Desertification

Poor farming practices are also taking their toll. The edges of China's deserts are creeping forwards, swallowing up fields and forests. This is known as desertification. Overgrazing of grassland and uncontrolled logging, made worse by drought, dry out the soil and turn it to dust.

⌄ Desertification is making areas uninhabitable in Inner Mongolia, China's third-largest province.

IN 2013 IN BEIJING, THERE WERE 60 DAYS ON WHICH THE AIR QUALITY WAS SAID TO BE HAZARDOUS TO LIFE.

FOCUS ON

☑ **BEIJING SMOG**

Thick, choking smog, created by chemicals from the city's power stations, factories, and five million cars, make Beijing a difficult place to live in. Pollution regularly hits ten times the World Health Organisation's recommended maximum level. In 2015, four coal-burning power stations around Beijing were closed down to try to stop things getting worse.

⌄ People in Beijing wear masks as protection against the smog (right).

23

MEGACITIES

U ntil a few decades ago, most people in China lived in the countryside and worked the land. Today, half live in cities, and tens of millions more are joining them every year. By the year 2030, as people find it ever harder to make a living by farming, it is likely that more than a billion Chinese will be city dwellers.

∧ Hong Kong's 7 million people are packed in to 1000 sq km of space.

∨ Many of Shanghai's residents live in towering skyscrapers.

City sizes

City populations in China are huge. In 2015, when the population of London, the UK's largest city, was 8.6 million, China had seven 'megacities', with more than 10 million inhabitants (see table). There are a further 90 cities with populations of 5-10 million, and around 170 cities with populations between 1 and 5 million.

City	Population
Shanghai	25.4 million
Beijing	21.6 million
Guangzhou	12.7 million
Shenzhen	12.3 million
Tianjin	11.0 million
Chongqing	10.0 million

Building boom

Towering apartment blocks are springing up by the thousand in cities to house all the people flocking in from the countryside to work in factories. Entire new cities are being planned and built. Some of these cities look like ghost towns – they are ready but empty, waiting for people to move in.

⌃ These new appartments are being built in Dalian City.

FOCUS ON

✓ **SHANGHAI**

China's biggest city is Shanghai, a global financial and commercial centre, and major port. Shanghai is one of the world's most modern cities, with busy streets, expensive shops, bars and restaurants. Tallest of the city's glimmering skyscrapers is the Shanghai Tower, at 632m.

≫ The Shanghai Tower

BEIJING

With more than 21 million people, China's capital, Beijing, is pretty crowded. It is the country's political and cultural centre, and its main transportation hub.

Holiday highlights

Some 4.5 million foreign tourists visit Beijing each year to see the city's historical sights. Top destinations are the palace complex of the Forbidden City, Tiananmen Square (right), the Summer Palace (above right), the Olympic Park with its Bird's Nest Stadium (below right), and the Great Wall (see page 30). The best way to get around is by underground train, or by bike, if you're feeling brave!

⌄ Busy Beijing streets and modern malls

Tiananmen Square

Tiananmen Square, in the city centre, is the size of 90 football pitches and the world's largest public square. At its heart is the mausoleum of Chairman Mao, the first leader of the People's Republic of China, who died in 1976. Join the long queue to catch a glimpse of his embalmed body.

⌃ Mao's mausoleum

FOCUS ON

☑ **THE FORBIDDEN CITY**

This huge palace complex was built for Emperor Yongle in the fifteenth century, and remained a royal residence for 500 years. It has more than 800 buildings, and a staggering 9,000 rooms. It got its nickname because ordinary Chinese people were forbidden to go inside.

IT TOOK A MILLION WORKERS MORE THAN 14 YEARS TO BUILD THE FORBIDDEN CITY.

« Beijing's famous Forbidden City

GROWING UP IN CHINA

The one-child policy means that many Chinese children grow up without brothers or sisters. Despite this, family is very important. Family celebrations are treasured in China, and great respect is shown to parents and grandparents.

⌃ Children and their teacher salute the Chinese flag at the start of the school day.

City and country living

Housing varies widely across China. In cities, where land space is limited, families often live in high-rise buildings. In the countryside, homes are more traditional and, often, more basic. They may be arranged around a courtyard, shared with a few of the family's animals.

« Rural homes

⌃ Village life in Guilin, China – walking past the pigsty!

Life lessons

Officially, China is an atheist country but the three ancient religions of Buddhism, Taoism, and Confucianism are still very important. The teachings of Confucius, a philosopher who lived between 551 and 479 BCE, still guide the lives of many Chinese people today, at work, at home and at school.

BY THE AGE OF NINE, CHINESE CHILDREN NEED TO BE ABLE TO READ AND WRITE ABOUT 2,000 CHARACTERS.

⌃ Buddhist monks at a monastery in China.

FOCUS ON

 IN THE CLASSROOM

Education is very important in China. Basic education is paid for by the government. Children spend up to 12 hours a day in class, often six days a week, with two breaks for meals. They are expected to work hard and behave well. They often feel a great deal of pressure to succeed. Parents who push their children to do well at school are known as tiger parents.

⌃ Students sitting an exam outside in the woods

WALLS AND WARRIORS

China's amazingly rich and ancient culture stretches back thousands of years. For much of its history, it was ruled by powerful emperors. The first, Emperor Qin Shi Huang, united China as one country and was responsible for two of China's greatest sites: the Great Wall and the Terracotta Army.

⌃ Each year the Great Wall attracts 10 million visitors.

The Great Wall

The Great Wall of China snakes for thousands of kilometres across the country. It isn't a single wall, but a whole system of walls linked together. It was originally built from earth and rocks in the third century BCE by Emperor Qin Shi Huang, to keep out raiders from the north. It's the biggest man-man structure on Earth, but it can't be seen from the Moon, despite the legend.

⌄ A section of Great Wall, complete with watchtowers

Clay army

In 1974, farmers digging a well near the city of Xian in central China made a staggering discovery when they unearthed an army of thousands of life-sized clay warriors, horses and chariots. Known as the Terracotta Army, it was made to guard Emperor Qin Shi Huang's tomb. Each of the warriors has beautifully detailed clothes and facial features – and no two are the same.

≪ Each soldier has an individual face.

⌄ The mighty Terracotta Army

THE UNDERGROUND VAULT THAT CONTAINS THE TERRACOTTA ARMY MEASURES 230 METRES BY 60 METRES — THE SAME AREA AS TWO FOOTBALL PITCHES.

FOCUS ON

☑ **BUILDING THE GREAT WALL**

The emperor forced hundreds of thousands of slave labourers to work on the Great Wall, and many of them died. Only small sections of the original wall remain but new sections are sometimes found, mostly in remote desert or forest regions.

GETTING ABOUT IN CHINA

China is an enormous place to get around but, in recent years, the goverment has invested heavily in new, faster railways and roads to link its expanding cities and carry its growing number of cars. Despite this, many Chinese still rely on a more traditional form of transport – the bike.

⌃ The Jiaozhou Bay Bridge

» Ultra-modern high speed trains have transformed China's railways.

New trains

China's trains are fast, efficient, and, usually, on time. A huge network of tracks, covering more than 100,000km, connects the big cities, and links China to its neighbours. Ultra-modern C- and G-class trains have a top speed of 350 km per hour.

≫ A packed train on the Shanghai subway, the third longest in the world

FOCUS ON

✓ CHINA'S BICYCLES

The streets of China's towns and cities once thronged with millions of bicycles. But cycling to work has declined sharply with the growth of car use. Even so, electric bikes are becoming popular with commuters fed up with being stuck in the traffic jams.

>> Bikes are used to carry heavy loads!

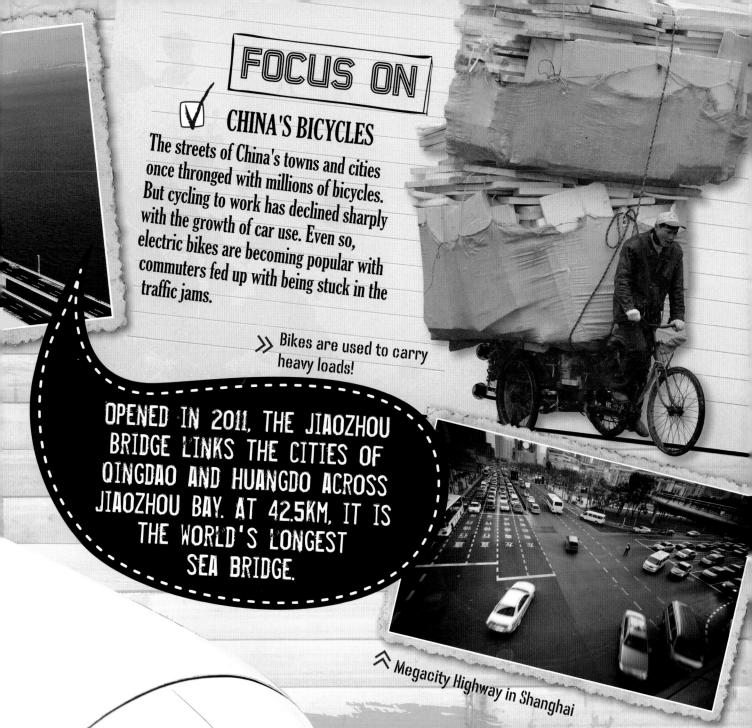

OPENED IN 2011, THE JIAOZHOU BRIDGE LINKS THE CITIES OF QINGDAO AND HUANGDO ACROSS JIAOZHOU BAY. AT 42.5KM, IT IS THE WORLD'S LONGEST SEA BRIDGE.

⌃ Megacity Highway in Shanghai

City transport

Thousands of cars, buses, trucks, bicycles, motorbikes, and pedal-powered and motorised taxis jostle for space on the city streets. New metro lines, both over- and underground, are springing up in many of cities, to reduce traffic congestion and pollution.

DUMPLINGS AND DUCK

From noodles and yak meat in the west, to rice and seafood in the east, Chinese cuisine is vast and varied. Rice, meat, fish and noodles are staples but there are more unusual, ingredients to challenge your tate buds, such as fried locusts, ducks' tongues and birds' nest soup.

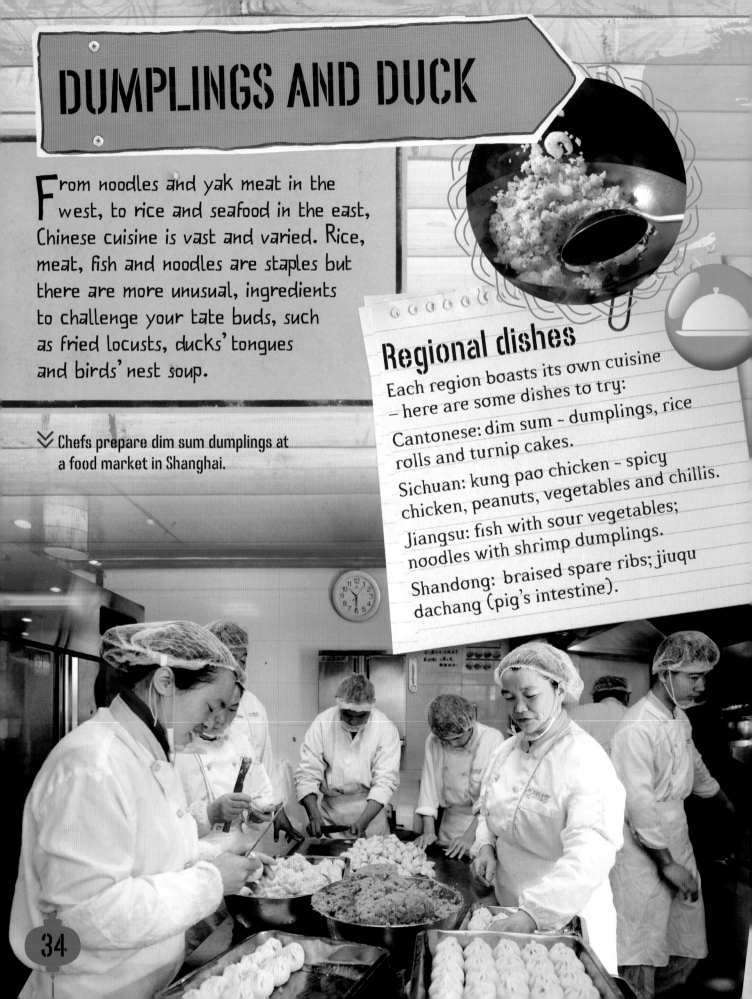

⌄ Chefs prepare dim sum dumplings at a food market in Shanghai.

Regional dishes

Each region boasts its own cuisine – here are some dishes to try:

Cantonese: dim sum – dumplings, rice rolls and turnip cakes.

Sichuan: kung pao chicken – spicy chicken, peanuts, vegetables and chillis.

Jiangsu: fish with sour vegetables; noodles with shrimp dumplings.

Shandong: braised spare ribs; jiuqu dachang (pig's intestine).

Peking duck

Crispy strips of roast duck meat and skin, called Peking duck, is one of China's most famous dishes, and is a speciality of Beijing (Peking was the old name for Beijing). A favourite dish in the Forbidden City, the duck is often served wrapped in pancakes, along with cucumber and bean sauce.

›› Peking duck is a favourite dish in Chinese restaurants.

IN MOST CHINESE RESTAURANTS OUTSIDE CHINA, THE FOOD SERVED IS CANTONESE.

FOCUS ON

☑ STREET FOOD

The packed streets of China's cities are lined with small food stalls, selling an amazing variety of street snacks (known locally as 'little eats'). Each region and city has its own speciality street food. Popular in Shanghai is xiao long bao, steamed dumplings filled with thin soup.

HAVE YOU EATEN YET?

Food is such a big part of Chinese life that people often greet each other with 'Have you eaten yet?' rather than 'How are you?' Dinner guests help each other by filling each other's bowls and teacups, and there are plenty of toasts to the host.

IT IS CONSIDERED THE HEIGHT OF RUDENESS TO POINT AT A FELLOW DINER WITH YOUR CHOPSTICKS!

⌄ Most Chinese children are chopstick experts by the age of five.

Chopsticks and bowls

Chinese people eat with chopsticks rather than knives and forks, and only use a spoon for eating soup. Food is normally eaten from small bowls (below) rather than plates.

Eating a meal

A traditional Chinese meal is made up of two different elements, in carefully balanced proportions. The first element, called fan, is made up of rice, noodles or dumplings. The second element, called tsai, is made up of meat and vegetables, and brings flavour to the meal.

Sharing food is an important part of Chinese family life.

FOCUS ON

✓ **DRINKING TEA**

Tea drinking was probably invented in China, and brewing and drinking tea is still very important. Tea is part of every Chinese meal, and people visit teahouses to socialise. There are lots of different teas to choose from, including white tea, green tea, black tea, and a variety called oolong.

SPORTING CHINA

China is famous for its martial arts, which are still practised as a way of keeping fit. Basketball, badminton and table tennis are also popular. And, like everyone else, the Chinese love football!

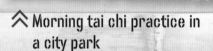

⤊ Morning tai chi practice in a city park

Morning exercises

Keeping fit is important to the Chinese, and most people do some form of regular exercise – perhaps a trip to the gym, or more traditionally, a session of martial arts. This often takes the form of an early morning trip to the local park to practise tai chi with friends and neighbours.

ZHANG SANFENG, FOUNDER OF TAI CHI, WAS SAID TO BE SO FIT THAT HE COULD WALK AROUND 350 MILES A DAY!

>> Chinese table tennis aces competing against Japan for the gold medal at the 2012 Olympics.

Martial arts

A dizzying array of martial arts is practised in China. There are hundreds of fighting styles. Some are fast and athletic; others use slow, controlled movements. Many styles originate from Shaolin Monastery in Henan province, where monks have practised martial arts since the seventh century CE.

FOCUS ON

☑ THE BEIJING OLYMPICS

In 2008, Beijing played host to the Summer Olympic Games. Chinese athletes won 51 gold medals. The hub of the Games was the National Stadium, nicknamed the Bird's Nest, which is now a tourist attraction and concert venue. Many of the 2008 venues will be re-used in 2022, when Beijing hosts the Winter Olympics.

⌄ The spectacular Olympic opening ceremony in the Bird's Nest, Beijing in 2008

⌃ Young monks practising kung fu at Shaolin Monastery

ART AND MUSIC

Can you imagine your handwriting being framed and displayed in a gallery? In China, calligraphy (the art of handwriting) is highly admired, as are other traditional arts, such as landscape painting and porcelain making.

⌃ This porcelain vase dates from the Ming dynasty.

⌃ A traditional painting in ink of mountains and trees

Landscape painting

The mountains, forests and rivers of the landscape often feature in traditional Chinese art. Like calligraphy, these paintings are done in ink, on paper or silk, with simple brush strokes. They are often mounted on scrolls. Artists paint imaginary places, emphasising the harmony of the natural world. The Chinese believe that looking at paintings of mountains is good for the soul.

⌃ Prepare to be dazzled at the Chinese opera!

Chinese opera

A night at the opera in China will leave you reeling. Dating back hundreds of years, Chinese opera is a mix of dance, music, acrobatics, fire-eating, martial arts, elaborate costumes and dramatic make-up, all rolled into one dazzling spectacle. Prepare to be amazed!

THERE ARE CALLIGRAPHY COMPETITIONS IN CHINESE PARKS, USING WATER ON PAVING STONES, INSTEAD OF INK ON PAPER.

FOCUS ON

✓ **WRITTEN ART**

A traditional calligrapher works with paper, brush, ink stone and ink stick. These are known as the 'four treasures of the scholar'. Artists use all sorts of brushstrokes to form Chinese characters, and the strokes for each must be painted in a set order. Getting it right takes years of practice!

FESTIVALS AND HOLIDAYS

There are hundreds of festivals and holidays throughout the year in China. They're as much a part of the culture as silk-making and calligraphy. Some are celebrated across the whole country while others are marked locally.

Dancing dragons

Chinese New Year is celebrated in January or February with colourful festivities, including the dramatic dragon dance. To prepare for this important holiday people clean to get rid of bad luck and buy new clothes and shoes to symbolise a new start. Special foods are eaten, such as niangao (New Year's rice cake) and dumplings, which are symbols of wealth.

⊼ At New Year, China's streets are decorated with red lanterns and banners.

Lantern Festival

Fifteen days after New Year, the Lantern Festival marks the end of the celebrations. Red lanterns, to symbolise good fortune, are lit. People solve riddles printed on them and feast on sticky rice balls, their round shape representing family togetherness.

⌃ Lanterns come in all shapes and sizes.

AT NEW YEAR, CHILDREN ARE GIVEN GIFTS OF MONEY IN RED ENVELOPES. THE COLOUR RED IS THOUGHT TO BE LUCKY IN CHINESE CULTURE.

FOCUS ON

☑ ICE AND SNOW FESTIVAL

Each year, hundreds of thousands of people brave freezing temperatures to attend the annual Ice and Snow Festival in the city of Harbin. Highlights of the festival are the enormous ice sculptures, carved from blocks of ice from the river. People use saws, chisels and picks to transform the ice into scenes from Chinese fairytales, or famous world sights, such as the Great Wall, Egyptian pyramids and Niagara Falls.

⌃ Harbin's dramatic ice sculptures

21st CENTURY CHINA

China's rapid growth into an economic superpower has created a country with many challenges. While some people are making money, many others, especially in the countryside, remain desperately poor. And, while the government encourages entrepreneurs, it also strictly controls Internet use.

⌃ Workers install panels at a solar power station in Sichuan province.

Greener China

China is responsible for more than a quarter of the world's carbon emissions, which come mostly from its coal-fired power stations. The Chinese government has come under pressure from the rest of the world to cut emissions, and has introduced emission targets, as well as a programme of renewable energy projects.

Modern and ancient

Despite China's march towards becoming a modern country, tradition remains very important to the Chinese. The contrast between modern and ancient is one of China's most striking features. So, as bankers trade on computers in new offices, in the park below, people practise the slow movements of tai chi.

⌃ Elderly residents at a social welfare home, dressed in traditional blue 'Mao suits'.

CHINA IS AIMING TO HAVE ITS OWN SPACE STATION BY THE 2020s, AND EVENTUALLY LAND TAIKONAUTS ON THE MOON.

FOCUS ON

☑ **CHINA IN SPACE**

China is keen to make its mark in space, and catch up with the successes of the USA, Russia, India and Europe. In 2003, China became only the third country to put a human into space, on the Shenzhou 5 mission. Chinese astronauts (called taikonauts) have also visited the International Space Station.

QUIZ

How much do you know about China's land and people? Try this quick quiz and find out!

1) What is the capital city of China?
a) Shanghai
b) Beijing
c) Lhasa

2) How many people live in China?
a) 1.4 billion
b) 1.4 million
c) 100,000

3) What is the name of China's highest mountain?
a) Huangshan
b) Mount Kailash
c) Mount Everest

4) Which of these Chinese animals are extinct?
a) Baiji
b) Giant panda
c) Red-crowned crane

5) Which crop is grown in paddy fields?
a) Tea
b) Rice
c) Potatoes

6) Where does silk come from?
a) Mines
b) Plants
c) Moths

7) Whose body can you see in Tiananmen Square?
a) Emperor Qin Shi Huang
b) Chairman Mao
c) Confucius

8) How many children do most Chinese families have?
a) One
b) Two
c) Three

9) What are dim sum?
a) Chinese shoes
b) Chinese paintings
c) Chinese dumplings

10) Chinese people eat food with
a) Their fingers
b) Knives and forks
c) Chopsticks

11) Which of these isn't a martial art?
a) Kung fu
b) Chinese opera
c) Tai chi

12) What is Harbin famous for?
a) Smog
b) Pandas
c) Ice

True or false
a) Table tennis is the unofficial national sport of China.
b) The Great Wall of China can be seen from the Moon.
c) Nearly 300 languages are spoken in China.

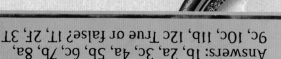

Answers: 1b, 2a, 3c, 4a, 5b, 6c, 7b, 8a, 9c, 10c, 11b, 12c True or false? 1T, 2F, 3T

GLOSSARY

atheist
Someone who does not believe in God or gods.

calligraphy
The art of doing beautiful handwriting.

controversial
Describes something that causes people to have different opinions and to disagree.

dialect
A version of a language spoken in a particular place or by a particular group of people.

drainage basin
The area of land around a river from which water drains into the river.

effluent
Liquid waste from a factory or sewage works.

emission
Waste materials that are discharged from factories or sewage works.

endangered
An animal or plant that is in danger of becoming extinct.

ethnic group
A group of people that have many racial, cultural and religious features in common.

extinct
Describes an animal or plant that has died out.

gorge
A deep valley or ravine.

hydroelectric
Electrictiy that is made by the power of running water.

martial arts
Various techniques of self-defence and combat.

mausoleum
A large, stately tomb.

pilgrimage
A special journey made to a sacred (holy) place.

plateau
An area of level high ground.

porcelain
Very fine clay, used to make pots, vases and ornaments.

province
Some countries are divided into different regions, called provinces.

republic
When a country is governed by a president and politicians elected by the people.

wetlands
An area of marshy land.

Further information

Books

Unpacked: China by Susie Brooks (Wayland, 2015)

Food and Cooking Around the World: China by Rosemary Harkin (Wayland 2015)

Developing World: China and Beijing by Philip Steele (Franklin Watts, 2013)

Countries in Our World: China by Oliver James (Franklin Watts, 2013)

Countries Around the World China by Patrick Catel (Raintree, 2013)

Websites

www.lonelyplanet.com/China

A detailed travel guide to China.

www.gochina.about.com

Everything you need for planning a trip.

www.panda.org.cn/english

Watch pandas on the 24-hour webcam.

www.chinesenew years.info

All about Chinese New Year.

Index